PO FOLKS INVESTMENT GUIDE

Dr. PoFix

ISBN: 978-1-7165-0534-8 (sc)
ISBN: 978-1-7165-0533-1 (e)

Library of Congress Control Number: 2020920628

Lulu Publishing Services rev. date: 11/16/2020

This book is dedicated to my mother and father, Charles and Minnie Lewis, who taught me the real worth of a dollar, the value of hard work, and the joy of giving back.

A special thanks also goes to Sandra Lewis (wife), Tanya Lewis (daughter) and Jasmine Lewis (niece) for their moral support and assistance in helping me complete this book.

Preface

The longest journey begins with a first step.

- Chinese Proverb

Congratulations! You have taken the first step to reach your financial goals, and this guide will lay a seamless pathway to reach your financial destination.

Simply stated: *Po Folks Investment Guide* was written to help people with no money find money and invest it. It's really that simple.

Po Folks Investment Guide is designed for everyone. Whether you start with one dollar or a thousand dollars, you can follow this approach and build your financial wealth.

Before we go further, let me share a little something about my background. I am Lem Lewis. I was born in Lynchburg, Virginia, and attended college in Charlottesville, Virginia. I have a BA in economics and an MBA. During my career, I have been a licensed stockbroker, an insurance broker, a real estate broker, and I worked in international and corporate finance at Wachovia Bank. I spent thirty years with Landmark Communications in a number of financial and operating roles and retired as corporate executive vice president and chief financial officer. I have served on several corporate boards of major Fortune 500 companies.

Usually, when people share their backgrounds like this, it is to establish credibility. For you, the main takeaway is that I have two college degrees and I've been around a lot of smart people. However, that does not guarantee that I know anything about investing money.

There you have it, the first lesson of this guide: know who you're dealing with.

This guide assumes you know little to nothing about investing and that you have little or no money to invest. For a large percentage of people, this has been true at one time or another. (If this is not true for you and you have either a lot of knowledge and/or a lot of money, please feel free to share both with us.)

This guide is about two concepts: (1) how to create or find money so you have some to invest and (2) after you have money available to invest, what to do with it. This guide is *not* about how to get rich quickly in the stock market or how to invest in a bunch of exotic or questionable financial instruments. Simply stated, what this guide *will* do is help you improve your financial well-being or wealth over a period of time. It was created to help people of modest means become people of more substantive means.

Growing up, I remember old folks saying, "It is not how much money you make, but what you do with it that counts."

This statement will be like the Pledge of Allegiance for users of this guide. It will be our mantra. It will appear at the end of each chapter, and it will be the final words of this guide.

So, are you ready? Let's get started.

Chapter 1

The Chicken vs. the Egg Dilemma

The best time to plant a tree was twenty years ago. The next best time is now.

—Author Unknown

In life, there are many examples of the chicken vs. the egg dilemma. "Which came first, the chicken or the egg?" There have been decades of discussion, argument, and debate around this very simple question.

It's the same for po folk when it comes to investments, but with a more concrete answer. Why don't po folk invest? Why are po folk poor? There is one unassailable truth: they have no money. At least no money to invest.

As with the chicken vs. egg discussion, we have to resolve this real issue. We do that by clearly and unequivocally stating the obvious: one must have money to invest money. (I know that's hard for people with money to comprehend, but it's fairly basic for those without money looking to make their first investment.)

Since most people's budgets are tight and they don't have money to invest, *Po Folks Investment Guide* will teach you where to get free money to invest.

The important part of this solution is that it's controlled by us and not dependent on anyone or anything else. It is totally within our grasp and easily achievable.

What is this "aha moment" that will bestow all of this free money upon us? It is simply a combination of knowing what to look for in your current budgets and changing a few behaviors.

Of these two, changing the behaviors of how you *think* about and spend money is the most important part of this guide.

Ultimately, there is absolutely nothing more important than this: Change how you think about money!

In Chapter 2, we talk about changing how you think about money, how you change your behaviors about money, and how you find "hidden" money in your existing budget. These hidden savings can then be captured and redeployed in assets (investments) that go up or appreciate in value.

Next up—Two Buckets: Consumption vs. Investments.

It is not how much money you make—
it's what you do with it that counts!

Chapter 2

Consumption vs. Investment

A penny saved is a penny earned!

This is the most important chapter in this guide. Let me repeat that: this is the most important chapter in this guide.

Why? Because this is the chapter where you have to: (1) acknowledge existing unproductive behaviors and (2) change those behaviors.

This is also the chapter where you see how understanding one simple concept can change your financial future forever. Get this right, and you have mastered the secret of wealth creation.

There are many things in life that you can always count on. A few we may agree on: gravity, aging, death, taxes, and change. Add to this list people's desire to have things—the more things the better. This has been true since the beginning of time and probably always will be true.

You often see articles about entertainers and sports figures who made millions of dollars and now are filing for bankruptcy. You have probably wondered how someone who has earned $50 million, $100 million, or $200 million could possibly go bankrupt. One would think that a person would have to try really hard to blow that kind of money. Yet almost weekly we read about some celebrity doing just that, blowing millions of dollars.

It would appear that wanting and acquiring things scales with the amount of money available to purchase those things. A person who makes $30,000 a year has less money available to purchase things, but purchase they do. The items may not be as expensive as the purchases of a person who makes $100,000, but the behaviors are the same.

Simply stated, the more money people have, the more things and types of things they can and do buy. Po Folk buy fewer things and less expensive things, but they still buy. Consumption is as American as apple pie. It exists at all levels of society and in almost every culture.

So, this chapter is about pulling back the curtain on wealth creation so anyone can understand the basics needed to create wealth. We call this basic concept *two buckets,* the twin buckets of consumption vs. investments. It is these two buckets that our Dr. PoFix icon on our front cover is carrying, and it is an understanding of these two buckets that, if mastered, will help create the wealth you so desire.

Two Buckets: Consumption vs. Investments

Consumption

Consumption comes from the word *consume.* Anything you consume is gone! Gone as in never to return, gone as in worth nothing, or gone as in disappeared. Take your pick. I like to think of it as going to zero.

In life, there are many things that go to zero, and unfortunately a number of them are essential. Food is a great example. Although we all love it and we need it to live, once you consume it, it's gone forever. Another great example is the automobile. We need it to go to and from work, to shop, and to carry us to places we either need or want to go. However, from the day you buy most cars, *the minute the title changes to your name,* the obsolescence starts. You love it while it's new, shiny, and dependable, but one day it too eventually goes to zero. The amount you paid for the car, plus interest, plus maintenance, plus, plus, plus. You get the idea. As for your money, it is gone, never to appear again, just like vapor.

So, you ask, what's a person to do? We must have food, transportation, clothing, and a whole host of other things to survive.

Answer: Spend what you have to spend but no more. Buy used cars instead of new cars, and then drive them until they won't run anymore. I bet that got your attention! Please don't stop reading.

How many handbags do you really need? How many pairs of shoes do you really need? How many—feel free to finish the sentence. I think you get the point. Food is necessary, but eating out several times a week is not. So dine out occasionally, but eat at home most of the time and pack a lunch. It is much cheaper and probably a lot healthier. (These are just a few suggestions, and many more will be covered in the next chapter.)

Investment

Simply put, an investment is something that increases in value. All investments are made with the hope they will be worth more in the future than they were on the day of purchase. Some do, but unfortunately, some don't. However, very few will go to zero. Real estate, stocks, bonds, diamonds, gold, antique cars, etc. are all volatile, but they almost never go to zero. There are whole industries around each of these asset classes to help you navigate the ups and downs, but if properly managed, most of these assets should increase in value over time.

The main difference between consumption items and investment items is this: consumption items at the end of their cycle go to zero and investment items go up in value. Another way to look at this distinct difference is that investments work for you and therefore increase in value. People buy stocks, bonds, antique cars, gold, and a host of other value-generating assets because they know that historically they have been a store of value (an asset that maintains its value without depreciating). So, when you have an asset that creates value, and someone else is willing to pay for it, you normally have an asset that helps increase wealth. Good companies and real estate are two examples that historically have grown in value and are often sold at a profit.

What are the takeaways from this chapter? Just remember the farmer and his two buckets. The consumption bucket is beaten up, scratched, rusty, and probably leaks. It, therefore, will not hold water (value). Everything that goes in comes out. Contrast that with the investment bucket, which is in great shape, is not scratched or dented, and holds water (value). The message here? Put as little money in the consumption bucket as possible, and divert as much money as you can to the investment bucket, where it will grow in value.

Wealth creation begins with these two buckets. Understand and practice their roles, and you can increase your wealth.

Starting today, decide in which bucket you'll place each of your hard-earned dollars. Will it be bucket number one (consumption) or bucket number two (investment)? Finding the money is the easy part (see the next chapter); having the discipline to place it in the right bucket is the hard part. Make this determination every day with every dollar. It is your money, and you make all the decisions regarding it. Each dollar will go into one bucket or the other. Your decision.

J. Paul Getty, one of the world's wealthiest men in the twentieth century, knew what he was talking about when he said, "Watch your pennies, and the dollars will take care of themselves."

It is not how much money you make—
it's what you do with it that counts!

Chapter 3

Where Do We Get the Money to Invest?

*Almost every man knows how to earn money, but
not one in a million knows how to spend it!*

—Henry David Thoreau

Now that we understand the difference between consumption
and investment, we can get to work on our next big challenge—where do we get the money to invest?

First, it is important to understand what to do and what not
to do with our money. We can start our search for what I call
"free money."

Free money is money you free up in your existing budget—
money that is not being spent in the most productive ways.
That's not easy for most people, but it's often very surprising
when you discover you can come up with a few dollars here
and there and then redeploy that money to more efficient use.

In order to find free money, it is helpful to know how much you
are currently spending and on what. Over a period of several
years and in talking with many people, I have not found one
person who did not have free money in his or her existing
budget.

So, where is it, and how do we find it?

A great place to start is to track your expenditures for one week. Often when I mention budgeting, everyone in the room groans. I get it! So let's not jump right into budget keeping and instead do something simple. All you need is a pen or pencil and a piece of paper.

Starting on a Monday morning and continuing for one week, jot down every time you spend money, what you purchased, and where. It is important to do this for *every* transaction. Record all expenditures, whether they were made with cash, debit or credit cards, or checks.

At the end of the week, enter your expenditures into various categories: food, clothing, personal expenditures like haircuts, gas for your car, and any other heading you'd like to add. Now review what you spent—and where. That's it.

Here are a few questions to ask yourself:

- What items were necessary? Obviously, things like food, gasoline, electric bills, and other household expenses are necessary.

- What items were impulse items? Hint: $1.89 soda at the gas station, $8 for a small box of popcorn at the theater.

- Did you buy generic or brand names?

- What items were purchased because they were on sale and not because you really needed them? Example: You went to a department store to buy socks but saw this great handbag that was 25 percent off the regular price, so you snatched it up.

There are many other questions, but what we want to do is to identify purchasing behaviors that are reducing your bucket of free money.

Budgets

Everybody hates budgets, and nobody wants one. Most people treat them like diets. How can you possibly live your life measuring calories in three ounces of this or two portions of that every day? No wonder only the very disciplined are successful at dieting, and even then, the lost pounds are normally put back on. Budgets also can be like dieting—it's great when you start one, but you quickly grow tired of tracking every penny.

Trust me on this one—you need to start a budget because you have to know where your money is going. Once you know this, you can put your budget aside, at least temporarily. How is a budget different from a diet? We make it easy for you by providing a handy, ready-made blank budget.

Go to PoFolksInvestmentGuide.com, click on Budgets, and log in. We have prepared a budget sheet that you can easily fill out as you complete your purchases. Our guide also works on your phone.

Once you've tracked what you've bought for a week, you may want to see the big picture and keep a record of what you've spent in each major category for an entire month. Once you have done this, use the graphics on our budget sheet to see where your money is going, what you're spending it on, and where there are opportunities for creating free money.

Budget Worksheets

At the back of this book is a one-page budget worksheet (appendix 1). I have reproduced it below for our discussion. It is extremely simple and will capture most of the income and expenses for the average person. If you have additional expense categories that are not listed, there is a place where they can be added.

Exhibit 1
Monthly Budget Worksheet

Category	Budget	Actual	Difference	Notes
Monthly pay (after taxes)				
Other				
Total Monthly Income				
Flexible Expenses	**Flexible expenses** are costs that are easily changed, reduced or eliminated. Spending money on entertainment and clothing represent **flexible expenses**. Even **expenses** that must be incurred, such as a grocery bill, can be considered **flexible** because the amount spent can vary.			
Utilities				
Electricity/gas/phone				
Other				
Total Utility Expenses				
Food and Entertainment				
Groceries/dining out				
Other				
Total Food and Entertainment				

On your budget worksheet there are 3 columns with the headings: Budget, Actual, and Difference. An example of a Budget category: You plan to spend no more than $140 for lunch for the month of September (20 business days a month x $7.00 per day.) Let's say you spend only $100 for the month (Actual), then your Difference between Budget and Actual is $40.00.

Congratulations, in September, you saved an extra $40.00 for your Investment Bucket. Trust me, nothing bad will happen to you if you continue to do this forever, and not only for lunch but for any of your other major expense categories as well.

Transportation				
Gas/parking/tolls				
Other				
Total Transportation Expenses				
Children				
School/lessons/ clothing				
Other				
Total Children Expenses				
Personal				
Dry cleaning/personal grooming				
Other				
Total Personal Expenses				
Health				
Doctor's visits/ medications				
Other				
Total Health/Medical Expenses				
Savings/Other Expenses				
Savings (401k, IRA)				
Other				
Total Savings/Other Expenses				
Total Flexible Expenses				
Fixed Expenses	A fixed expense is "any expense that does not change from period to period," such as mortgage or rent payments, some utility bills, and loan payments. The amounts may vary slightly, but you know they are due on a regular basis.			

Housing				
Mortgage/rent/ insurance/taxes				
Other				
Total Housing Expenses				
Utilities				
Cable/internet				
Other				
Total Utility Expenses				
Health				
Insurance premiums				
Other				
Total Health/Medical Expenses				
Transportation				
Car payments/ insurance				
Other				
Total Transportation Expenses				
Loan/Other Payments				
Student loans/alimony				
Other				
Total Loan/ Other Expenses				
Children				
Child care				
Other				
Total Children Expenses				

Total Fixed Expenses				
Monthly Totals				
Total Monthly Income				
Total Monthly Expenses				
Difference				

Before starting your budget, get a copy of the most recent statements for your checking and credit/debit card accounts and any other monthly records that track income and expenses.

You can do this for one week, but I recommend you try keeping a budget for a month. This one-time generated budget is all that is necessary for most people. Your daily/weekly activities are accumulated in your monthly statements and monthly budget. Since most companies rely on monthly budgets, your record-keeping similarly is made much easier.

You can see the worksheet captures all sources of income and expenses. To the best of your ability, note all of your monthly income (after-tax income, since that's all you have to spend) and monthly expenses. Your after-tax income is the amount of your paycheck or what is deposited in your bank for each pay period.

Your monthly income also includes any money that comes in the door such as Social Security and pensions.

On the expense side, the worksheet is divided into Fixed Expenses, such as car, rent, or mortgage payments, and Flexible Expenses, like gas/oil or electricity. Your electric bill probably is higher in winter and summer than in the spring and fall, when you use less heat and air conditioning. So take an average of what you normally spend over several months and use that for your electricity expense. Some months you will be over and some months you will be under. That's okay.

This one-time monthly budget is now the road map to your financial future, and it's where you'll find free money for investing. Believe me when I say it's there!

Now What?

Take some time to review your worksheet. Do your expenses exceed your income? Don't worry—this is true for most people. How much is the shortfall (expenses over income)?

Is this how you thought you were spending your money? Any surprises?

Let's recap. In chapter 2, you learned about consumption vs. investment and how consumption dollars go to zero and investment dollars go up or maintain their value, at a minimum.

Now look at your budget. If you are like most of us, very little goes into the investment bucket. The investment bucket represents your savings from sources like 401(k) programs or stocks (and we hope if you own stocks, they're going up in value, not down!) No savings? Pat yourself on the back and keep reading because the *Po Folks Investment Guide* can still help you improve.

A reminder: monthly income more often than not is locked in, at least for the short term, as are most fixed expenses. Both fixed income and fixed expenses are typically determined annually—like annual salary raises, a new apartment lease, or a new car payment. In the short run, we can do nothing about that, but we won't give up and throw in the towel.

So where will we look for free money? You guessed it—flexible expenses.

It is not how much money you make—
it's what you do with it that counts!

Chapter 4

Why Did I Do That? Behavioral Economics

Don't tell me where your priorities are. Show me where you spend your money, and I'll tell you what they are.

—James W. Frick

Flexible expenses is a catch-all phrase for a number of spending categories. It's everything that is not a fixed expense, and it's where most of your unplanned, impulse spending occurs. It's the consumption bucket, the biggest bucket there is.

In earlier chapters, we have mentioned behaviors both good and bad. The Flexible Expenses category has the worst behaviors and is the place where we will find most of our free money.

But first let's discuss a branch of economics called behavioral economics.

Have you ever purchased something (impulse buy), driven home, taken it out of the box, and asked yourself, "Now why did I just buy this?"

Have you purchased something you really didn't need, but because it was only five dollars, you said, "Oh, what the heck?"

Have you ever had a family member or a friend invite you to go somewhere or do something you really had no interest in, but you did it anyway because they wanted to do it?

Well, now you know what behavioral economics is all about. It is the study of people's behaviors as they relate to money. Economics is a social science (one plus one does not always equal two), and figuring out people's behaviors is a full-time job. Suffice it to say, control the "Why did I do that?" question, and two very important things will happen: (1) the Flexible Expenses category of your budget decreases significantly, and (2) free money is created for investment. The destruction of number one is the creator of number two.

Thus begins the flow of free investment money (money for investment).

Here are a few examples.

1. On a beautiful Saturday morning, I met a dear friend for coffee at one of our major hangouts, McDonald's. We both ordered coffee. My friend ordered a medium coffee with cream. The clerk asked if she wanted a specially priced coffee for senior citizens. My friend answered no. The clerk asked me what I wanted. I replied, "Small senior coffee with cream." My friend is a former investment advisor and is a very astute financial person.

    My small senior coffee was seventy-nine cents and her medium coffee was $1.49—a whopping seventy cents' difference. This McDonald's offered free refills with as many refills as you liked.

If, as some of my retired friends do, we did this every weekday morning, the saving would be considerable. In this case, the seventy cents' difference between her cup of coffee and my senior cup would amount to a savings of $3.50 per week. For fifty-two weeks, the annual savings would be $182. Let me repeat that—$182 a year! Cha-ching, I just found $182 of free money for my investment bucket.

By the way, I asked my friend why she didn't order the small senior coffee as I did. She blushed and said, "I am simply not ready to be a senior." Her age? Sixty-three. That is behavioral economics at its finest!

2. How many times have you been in a store or mall, walked past an attractive display, spotted something interesting, and before you knew it, you were standing in the cashier's line? The item likely had not been on your shopping list, nor had it even been a wishful thought. Rather, it caught your eye, and just like that, you had bought it. Then, once you arrived home, you had to think twice about what to do with it. So you tucked it in a corner out of the way, and that is where it stays until it goes to the attic or Goodwill.

This kind of wasteful expenditure is also listed under Flexible Expenses. Whether it cost one dollar, ten dollars, or one hundred dollars, we have all done this. Unplanned impulse buys are normally the most wasteful and almost always go to zero.

3. Another example of behavioral economics or "Why did I do that?" is our almost religious dedication to name brands. When shopping at your local grocery store, how many times have you passed by the store brand to buy the national brand? We have been taught through advertising and other means that the less-expensive store brand could not possibly be as good as the more recognized national brand. Inexpensive is called *cheap,* and with cheapness comes the expectation of less quality.

    These store brands often cost anywhere from 10 percent to 25 percent less than their better-known national brand competitors. A great way to test this theory is to price-check items in the healthcare area of your grocery store or in your local drugstore. For example, the next time you are in the grocery store, go to the cold medicine aisle and pick a bottle of any of the national brands. Somewhere very nearby will be the local or generic brand. Next, look at the list of ingredients. Then do the same for the generic or store brand. Not only will they almost always be the same, they are often listed in the same order on the labels.

    Now, chemistry being chemistry, the question posed by behavioral economics is: why are you paying more for the name brand? This behavior repeated hundreds of times a year can add up to hundreds of dollars of wasted expenditures—expenditures that go to zero.

Flexible Expenses is where we will find our free investment money for our investment bucket!

Some of you may think my next piece of advice is silly, so I want to acknowledge that. Here goes: find an old coffee can, old shoebox, old lard can, old sock, or old you-name-it container. Call it "My Investment Bucket."

When you find a way to save some money, take that savings home and put it in your bucket. I don't care if it's one cent, ten cents, one dollar, or a hundred dollars—put it in your bucket. If you have the savings in cash, put it in your bucket. Why am I asking you to do this? Because you want to remove it from your funds available to spend. Childish? Maybe. But it works!

In summary, you now know the difference between consumption and investment, you understand the concept of free investment money, and you know how behavioral economics and your own financial decisions, once changed, can create the money you need to fill your investment bucket.

Remember what J. Paul Getty said: "If you watch the pennies, the dollars will take care of themselves."

Some people find it helpful to record most of their expenses daily or weekly. If you really want to track every dime, this is a good way to do it. If not, do it at least once, and then repeat as often as you deem appropriate.

It is not how much money you make—
it's what you do with it that counts!

Chapter 5

There Are No Silver Bullets

Eat Well or Sleep Well, but Not Both … at Least Not Initially!

Every day, most of us see online offers and advertisements that say we can make money "the easy way." You can buy a lottery ticket for one dollar, and you *might* win a jackpot of millions of dollars. You can play the slot machines at a casino, and you *might* win millions of dollars. You can spend twenty dollars betting on a boxing match, and you *might* win thousands of dollars if your guy wins. You can sell tea on your social media account that is guaranteed to make people lose weight, and you *might* make thousands of dollars in profits in a week. With all of these examples, you have the opportunity to become rich with very little money to start. Tempting, right? But ask yourself one question: if all these schemes work so well, why isn't everyone who tries them rich?

These examples *might* produce high rewards but also high risks. Yes, if you buy a winning lottery ticket or play the slot machines in Las Vegas, you *might* win a million dollars by investing just a few dollars. The keyword for these chances is *might*. There's a possibility you'll win and a possibility you won't. There isn't any certainty. Do you know the probability of winning the Powerball lottery? It's about 1 in 292 *million*. Put another way, if you bought 292 million lottery tickets, you would win the jackpot about once. Your chances of being hit by lightning are about 1 in one million. How many people do you know who have been hit by lightning?

To summarize, when you invest your money in high-risk opportunities, there is a high risk you will lose it.

Gambling and get-rich-quick schemes have another downside. By now, you are using the two bucket tips and tools to change your budgeting and savings habits. You're probably beginning to see and save money you didn't know you had. After all of your hard work, why take a chance on a high-risk choice? A penny saved won't be a penny earned unless you invest it wisely.

There are no silver bullets for building your financial wealth. Just like with weight loss, slow and steady wins the race. A physician once told me that whatever I do to lose weight I will have to do the rest of my life to maintain it. Sure, you can lose ten pounds in one week by exercising for hours daily or barely eating. But can you continue to do that every day for a year to keep the pounds off? Her advice inspired me to focus on taking small steps toward healthy weight loss. The two buckets program is a low-risk approach with small steps, guaranteed to take you toward long-term financial success.

Once you put aside the idea of get-rich-quick tactics (which only help the people selling them), you can focus on the idea that time is on your side. The longer you save and invest wisely, the more money you will earn. Using this approach is how families with enormous wealth—millions and billions of dollars—keep it. Each member of the family contributes to the wealth, so it can build and build over many years until they don't have to worry about money any longer.

The next three chapters explain different ways you too can invest money wisely. But first, I'll explain the concept of risk. As you'll see, even slow and steady investment options have different levels of risk. Once you understand that, you can choose the ones that are best for you.

The Two Buckets Overview of Risk

In general, a financial investment gives you an opportunity to make money *with* your money. Each potential investment also comes with a level of risk or a chance you could lose money.

For most investment opportunities, it is hard to define the exact level of risk or the chance you could lose some or all of your money. That said, there are ways you can learn whether the risk for an investment is high, medium, or low. This is important because you should invest your money based in part on how much risk you're willing to take.

You may be comfortable with a high level of risk, but your best friend may be comfortable with a low level. Make your risk decisions on what's right for you.

Stocks vs. Bonds

Every day the stock market goes up or down. Most people know that it's good when the market goes up and bad when it goes down. Between these two opposites, most people get confused and either stay away from the stock market alto-gether or they put their money in a safe, secure bank or other conservative investment and sleep happily ever after.

The same is true with bonds, with the exception that bonds are even less well known, and the fog is even denser.

So, one of our key guidelines is to have more than a superficial knowledge of where and in what you invest. Spending time to understand what a share of stock really is and what a bond really represents lets you make informed decisions for your personal financial goals. Briefly stated, stocks are equity investments (ownership) in a company, and bonds represent debt (loans) to the company.

Here's an example of how equity (stocks) and debt (bonds) were used to start a company and the risks and rewards that came with them.

Bob's Furniture

Bob had been manager of a furniture store chain in the Midwest. He oversaw purchasing, sales, operations, and delivery for its three stores. Each store had been consistently profitable, even with increased competition over the years. Bob was well liked by the staff and was well known throughout his community as an all-around great guy. Bob had been general manager for more than ten years.

Bob had always wanted his own furniture store and decided to explore his dream. His decision to open his own store was accelerated when a building in a great location became available. After some preliminary work, Bob determined he would need approximately $1 million to open the store. The chart below shows how he obtained the money.

Bob's Furniture

Money needed to open store		$1,000,000
Equity (stock) down payment:		
Bob (50% of equity)	$100,000	
Cousin (25% of equity)	50,000	
Friend (25% of equity)	50,000	
Total equity (stock)	$200,000	
Loan (bond) interest only, 5 years @ 8%	800,000	
Total received		$1,000,000
Money used for:		
Building	250,000	
Inventory	500,000	
Working capital	250,000	
Total used		$1,000,000

To summarize, Bob raised $200,000 in equity (stocks) and borrowed $800,000 (bonds) in debt. The debt was provided by a bank, but it could have been placed with individuals (example: retirees) who needed annual income (interest) for living expenses. Bob would own 50 percent of the store, his cousin 25 percent, and his friend 25 percent.

Bob quit his longtime job and opened Bob's Furniture. It was an immediate success, and he had a great first year. After all expenses, including $64,000 of interest payments, the store netted $150,000. The next chart shows the equity value of each investors' holdings at the end of the first year.

	Original Investment +	Share of 1st Year Profits =	Total Value
Bob's value	$100,000	$ 75,000	$175,000
Cousin's value	50,000	37,500	87,500
Friend's value	50,000	37,500	87,500
Total at end of first year	$200,000	$150,000	$350,000

In his second year of business, the local economy was weaker, and Bob's Furniture cleared only $20,000 after expenses (including $64,000 of interest expense). So, at the end of the second year, the equity value of each investor was:

	Original Investment +	Share of 2nd Year Profits =	Total Value
Bob's value	$175,000	$ 10,000	$185,000
Cousin's value	87,500	5,000	92,500
Friend's value	87,500	5,000	92,500
Total at end of second year	$350,000	$ 20,000	$370,000

As you can see from the above scenarios, the equity shareholders' annual share of profits can vary greatly. During a good year, the equity shareholders do well, but in lean years, their share of profits can go down substantially. The opposite is true for the bondholders—the bank. It received $64,000 annually before any profits were paid to the equity investors.

So, would you rather be a bondholder or an equity investor? The bondholder gets a fixed amount each year, and the equity holder rides with the ups and downs (profitability) of the business.

Risk-takers often like the potential for greater gains or losses offered with an equity position, while more conservative investors like the certainty associated with a fixed return, or interest, on their investment. Some investors over time will have both stocks and bonds in their investment portfolios.

So, back to our chapter subtitle, "You can eat well or sleep well, but not both." Bondholders have less risk and therefore sleep well (at least theoretically). Equity holders eat very well some years and maybe not so well in other years.

There you have it—your choice!

(Although, in this chapter we only dealt with stocks and bonds and the risk associated with each, there are other types of investments that have different risk/return ratios. See graphic below for general risk/return scenarios. We use several asset classes, including bonds, stocks, and real estate. As the chart shows, the more risk you are willing to take, the higher return you should expect. Remember, the gold standard for safety is a bond issued by the United States government. As the graph shows, this is also the lowest return of the asset classes presented.)

It is not how much money you make—
it's what you do with it that counts!

Chapter 6

The World's Greatest Financial Concept

Compounding: Racing to Disaster
or Walking to Success

So far, we've covered two key concepts that are important on your two buckets journey. The first was to focus on finding and saving money. You can't invest if you don't have money to invest. More importantly, everyone can find money within their current budget to invest. Once you have money to invest, you should consider the second concept: risk. As I mentioned in the previous chapter, every investment involves some level of risk. The two buckets approach encourages you to know the risk and choose your investments based on your comfort level and goals.

Now that you have money (you didn't know you had) and you've assessed the appropriate level of risk for yourself, it's time to look at growing your money. If I told you that your money can begin making more money for you, would you believe me? This final concept for you to consider as you plan your investments is the ultimate reason *not to* put your savings in a shoebox in the closet or under a mattress.

Compounding

Our financial system has a lot of places you can put your money so it will grow after you have it. As demonstrated in chapter 5, some investors like a fixed, predictable rate of return (example: bond interest). For these investors, money grows based on compounding or compound interest, what some consider the greatest financial concept ever.

To explain compounding or compound interest, I'll start with the general idea of financial interest. Some financial accounts at your bank or savings institution apply interest to the amount you put in the account. Interest is the amount of money the banks add to your account based on how much money is in the account at a particular time. The interest is applied to your account at a specific rate or pace and is calculated during a particular time period (compounding frequency) and described in percentages. For example, the interest rate may be 1.0 percent and calculated monthly or 1.65 percent and calculated annually. Some common compounding frequencies are:

Daily—365 times per year

Weekly—52 times per year

Monthly—12 times per year

Quarterly—4 times per year

Semiannually—2 times per year

Annually—once per year

As far as your interest rate is concerned, banks must tell you the interest rate for your accounts or tell you how to find their current rates online.

Types of Interest Rates

There are two kinds of interest rates: simple and compound.

Let's consider a savings account with a simple annual rate of 3.0 percent. This means the investment (or how much is in the account before interest is applied) will grow by 3.0 percent by the end of one year. If you started with a $10 balance, by the end of the year, the balance would be $10.30. Thirty cents may not seem like a lot until you realize that you didn't have to do anything to get that extra money other than put ten dollars into your account. Now, imagine that your starting balance was $100 with a simple annual interest rate of 3 percent. At the end of the year, you would have $103. Let's take a look at this example over a period of five years.

Year	Balance ($)	Interest ($)	Ending Balance ($)
1	100	100 x .03 = 3	103
2	100	100 x .03 = 3	103 + 3 = 106
3	100	100 x .03 = 3	106 + 3 = 109
4	100	100 x .03 = 3	109 + 3 = 112
5	100	100 x .03 = 3	112 + 3 = 115

You started with $100, and your ending balance after five years is $115. One thing to note about a simple interest rate is that

it only applies to what you put into the account, or the principal. In the example above, at the start of the second year of
savings, your balance would be $103. With the same interest
rate, at the end of the year, the bank would add another $3 to
your account and your balance would be $106. Again, this is
a neat way to earn money for no additional work.

The second kind of interest is compounding interest. This
means that your interest earns more interest. Let's take the
same $100. With a 3 percent interest rate compounded annu-
ally (once a year), your balance would be $103 at the end of
the year. By the end of the second year, your balance would
be $106.09. This happens because the 3 percent compound
interest rate was applied to the $100 you put into the account
and the $3 in interest you earned from the previous year.
Another way to look at this is that your interest was earning
more interest for you. Let's take a look at this example over a
five-year period.

Year	Balance ($)	Interest ($)	Ending Balance ($)
0	100	100 x .03 = 3	103
1	103	103 x .03 = 3.09	106.09
2	106.09	106.09 x .03 = 3.18	109.27
3	109.27	109.27 x .03 = 3.28	112.55
4	112.55	112.55 x .03 = 3.38	115.93
5	115.93	115.93 x .03 = 3.48	119.41

By end of year five, you have $19.41 more than what you started
with, and all you had to do was put your money in the bank. Now
imagine this on a slightly bigger scale. Let's say you invest $1,000
for three years at 5 percent interest compounded annually.

Year	Balance ($)	Interest ($)	Ending Balance ($)
0	1,000	1,000 x .05 = 50	1,050
1	1,050	1,050 x .05 = 52.5	1,102.50
2	1,102.50	1,102.50 x .05 = 55.13	1,157.63
3	1,157.63	1,157.63 x .05 = 57.88	1,215.51

By the end of your third year, you have $215.51 more than you started with. Can you imagine what this will be if you leave it alone for twenty years or even thirty years? The longer you keep your money in this account, the more money you will have in the end. Can that shoebox under your bed do this for you? No! The idea is to place your money in the account long term and let it work for you. By the way, if you left the original $1,000 in the account at 5 percent interest for twenty years, you would have $2,653.30 (the original $1,000 plus $1,653.30 interest); after thirty years, you would have $4,321.94 (the original $1,000 plus $3,321.94 interest). Please see below what $10,000 earns at different interest rates and for different time periods.

Exhibit 3
Compound Interest
($10,000 Compounded at Various Rates/Various Time Periods)

Rate	5 Years	10 Years	15 Years	20 Years
5%	12,763	16,289	20,789	26,533
6%	13,382	17,908	23,966	32,071
7%	14,026	19,672	27,590	38,697
8%	14,693	21,589	31,722	46,610
9%	15,386	23,674	36,452	56,044
10%	16,105	25,937	41,772	67,275
11%	16,851	28,394	47,846	80,623
12%	17,623	31,058	54,736	96,463
13%	18,424	33,946	62,543	115,231
14%	19,254	37,072	71,379	137,435
15%	20,114	40,456	81,371	163,665

Simple Interest vs. Compound Interest

Although both types of interest will allow your money to grow, there are some differences between the two types, as you may have noticed. Compound interest is paid on the principal and all of the interest that you have earned. Simple interest is only paid on the principal. In the examples above, we started with a balance of $100, and by the end of the fifth year, our balance was a little larger with compounding interest than with simple interest. In other words, our return was higher when compounding the interest. In investing, compounding interest will allow your money to grow faster.

Now that you're taking your money out of the shoebox, you should be looking for an account with interest that compounds more frequently. If you already have a savings account, do you know how much interest you are earning? Take a look!

Bank Savings Accounts vs. Bonds

In chapter 5, we talked about Bob's Furniture Store. A bank had loaned him $800,000 at 5 percent simple interest for five years. Bank loans and bonds basically work the same way. Both are loans, and both can have a fixed rate of interest. Where they may differ is that bank loans normally have a shorter duration (term) than bonds. Bank loans usually are for five years or less, but bonds can have much longer timeframes—up to and including thirty years. Because bonds can have a longer maturity date, they may carry more risk (risk of payment and risk of inflation are two of the most obvious). Investors require a higher return (higher interest rate) to compensate for this added risk. Therefore, bonds generally carry a somewhat higher rate than bank loans. In fact, depending on various factors, it is not uncommon to see bonds with rates of 6 to 9 percent or more.

As an investor, the higher the interest rate, generally the more risk. Luckily for us, there are many bonds with many maturity dates and with different risk profiles, so we can choose one that fits our own risk and needs. Whether you invest for three years or thirty years, getting your money working for you through compounding is the ultimate goal.

Things to do:

Get more information about an account at your bank or savings institution.

- What is your current interest rate?

- Is it simple or compound?

- How often is it calculated? Daily, monthly, annually?

Shop around for the best bank or savings institution.

- If you can find an association with a higher interest rate calculated more frequently, your money can grow faster.

- Later we will examine investing in bonds, which generally have higher interest rates and longer maturities.

It is not how much money you make—
it's what you do with it that counts!

Chapter 7

Stocks, Bonds, or Both

One Size Does Not Fit All

Once you have some money to invest, you have to decide how to invest it. In chapter 5, we briefly outlined the risks and returns of stocks and bonds. For most people, four options will help you get started investing: savings accounts, stocks, bonds, or a mixture of these. The biggest decision you will have to make is "How much risk should I take?"

The money you have been saving from all of the techniques you learned in the previous chapters is the money you now get to invest. Many of the investment options outlined above can be started with as little as $25. The hard part is over—saving the first $25. You now have money in your investment bucket, and you can put it to work.

Let's get started by reviewing each of the four options with a comparison of risk and return for each of them. You can then decide where to make your very first investment.

Option 1: A Savings Account

Most people can go to a bank and open a savings account. To do that, you may have to deposit or give them a minimum amount of money ($25), which can be your first savings goal.

A savings account is a low-risk tool. As long as you have less than the balance ($250,000) that is insured by the Federal Deposit Insurance Corporation (FDIC) and you follow the rules for the account, your money is safe.

There are quite a few different types of savings accounts. You can have a basic savings account, which can be opened at most banks. Most times you can link your checking and savings accounts or just open a savings account. You will earn interest on the account, although it is not as high as some other options. You may have a certificate of deposit (CD), which typically offers a higher interest rate, but you are then committing to keep your money in the account for a specified period of time. This means you won't have access to the cash within that timeframe without paying a penalty. You can also have a money market account that typically offers a higher interest rate and usually requires a higher minimum balance than your basic savings account. These accounts generally have more limitations as well. There are also health savings accounts, retirement savings accounts, and many more. In Exhibit 4 I have listed several financial instruments, both short term and long term, with their interest rates. In general, the longer you are willing to lock up your savings (not available to you), the higher the expected return.

Usually, low risk comes with slower growth for your money. You might hear this described as "low risk, low return." Savings accounts usually have the lowest rates of growth of these investment options. For risk-averse investors, this option is one of the safest.

Option 2: Bonds

In chapter 5 (Bob's Furniture), we said another way that companies, governments, and other organizations raise money for operations and new projects is by issuing bonds. While a share of stock gives you part ownership of the company, a bond is a loan to the company. In exchange for the loan, the company or government promises to pay you back and to pay interest on the loan (just like a savings account). The organization issuing the bond has to tell you in advance when it will pay you back and at what interest rate.

Bonds are typically issued for long periods of time. Bonds (both government and corporate) sometimes have guarantees and/or are secured by the assets that are financed. Other bonds have no guarantees of any kind and are just "general obligation bonds" based on the creditworthiness of the borrower. Most bonds are longer term (more than five years) and carry a fixed rate of interest. This long-term nature of bonds introduces more risk, and to get an investor to assume more risk, the return (interest rate) has to be higher. As an example, a five-year bond may have a rate of 4 percent, a ten-year bond 5 percent, and a twenty-year bond 6.5 percent. (These examples are for illustrative purposes only, and rates will vary depending on the creditworthiness of the borrower, the term of the loan, and financial markets.)

In summary, bonds promise a specific rate of return, and they are usually offered by governments or organizations that pay them back. Bonds have more risk than savings accounts, and they are issued for longer periods of time. Therefore, they pay more (a higher interest rate) than an FDIC-insured savings account. Below is Exhibit 4 which shows the rates of different fixed income securities versus their risk and the time they are held.

Exhibit 4
Money Market/Fixed Income Rates
As of February 2019

Type	Rate
Money Market	0.18%
1 year Treasury	2.54%
5 year Treasury	2.52%
10 year Treasury	2.73%
5 year Corporate Bond	3.18%
10 year Corporate Bond	4.01%

Option 3: Stocks

In chapter 5, we said that some companies use shares, also known as stocks (or ownership claims), to raise money to pay for their business needs. When you buy stock in a company, you give them the price per share. In return, you expect the value of that stock to increase over time based on how well the company does. For example, let's say you buy one share of a company at the beginning of the year for ten dollars. If the company does well, the value of that share may be eleven dollars by the end of the year. If that happens, your investment would have gained 10 percent in value.

Stocks *prices* also can go down, like water running out of a leaky bucket. In fact, when a company liquidates or goes out of business, its stock value can go to zero. Thankfully, this does not happen often, but when it does, it can be financially very painful. Remember Woolworth's, Enron, and Pan American? They all closed their doors, and the price of their shares dropped considerably. Conversely, when a company does well, its shareholders do too. As you would expect, there can be a big gap between the two extremes. That means the risk is great.

Stock owners, also called shareholders, can also earn money through dividends. When a company makes a profit, they can put that money back into the company for operations or give it to their shareholders through dividend payments. Dividends are paid per share. For example, if the dividend payment is three dollars per share annually and you own five shares, your dividend payment would be fifteen dollars. Dividends may be in the form of cash, property, or even stock. With a stock dividend, if you own one hundred shares of a stock, and the company chooses to issue a 5 percent stock dividend, you would receive five additional shares of stock. Dividends are in addition to any appreciation in the stock price.

There is an entire industry dedicated to keeping track of the value of stocks for companies; it's called the stock market. You can read daily reports in newspapers, online, and even with apps on your phone to see whether the price of a stock you've purchased has gone up or down. If you aren't already familiar with stock reports—and even if you are—take a look at one online or in the newspaper. Pick a stock and look at its current value. You can even look to see what the value of a stock was ten years ago or even twenty years ago. In these reports, you can also look for a company that pays dividends to its share-holders. Look at how often the dividends are paid. There is much information that people can use to decide whether a particular stock is right for them.

Over time (there's that concept again), stocks can be a great investment. However, compared to a savings account, individual stocks may have substantially more risk. Even with the best information about a company that has a great track record, no one can be sure that its stock price will go up or down. On the other hand, a stock's price may grow faster and higher than the interest rate on a savings account. This makes investing in individual stocks a moderate to high-risk alternative, with moderate to above-average returns.

Again, every investment has some risk. While the stock market as a whole over time has grown in value (on average 7 to 9 percent over many decades), each individual company's stock may not. There is a chance or some risk that the stock you buy may go down in value over time and that you will lose some or all of your investment. So, while you may earn more with your money each year from investing in stock, compared to using a savings account, buying stock can be risky.

Option 4: Combination of Stocks and Bonds

One approach for investing money is to balance the best opportunities to earn a higher rate of growth against the risk of losing money. Remember that low-risk investments usually have low returns or slow growth, while investments with high returns and faster growth typically have a greater risk.

Many investors use a combination of investment tools to diversify their risk and earning potential. They choose a mix of low- and high-risk options to ensure they get some growth overall. For most of us, that means considering a mix of cash-like instruments (CDs), and stocks and bonds. One size does not fit all.

A general rule of thumb that some investors use is that the percentage of bonds in your portfolio should equal your age.

Example: Age 20 (Bonds 20%, Stock 80%); age 60 (Bonds 60%, Stock 40%), and so on. The thinking behind this general rule of thumb is as you grow older, you should take less risk than when you were younger. If you are twenty years of age and the market plummets, you may have many years to wait for its return; the opposite may not be true. So once again, your personal risk profile should play a role in your investment decisions.

It is not how much money you make—it's what you do with it that counts!

Chapter 8

Tools of the Trade

(Pay a Little, Get a Lot)

By now, you should have a greater appreciation for the difference between consumption and investment, you know how to find free money in your existing budget, and you have a better understanding of risk and reward. In the last two chapters, you learned about compounding (how fast your money grows) and the characteristics of equity (stocks) vs. debt (bonds). All of the above was the hard part—now we tackle a few tools of the trade.

For most of us, getting the money to invest was the hard part. For some, a greater fear is their lack of knowledge about what to do with it after they get it. Not to worry. There are millions of people with the same fears. Most people don't have the knowledge or the time to handle their investments. The more formidable of the two is ordinarily the lack of knowledge. The usual worry goes something like this: "I don't know what I'm doing, and I don't know who to trust."

One solution is the mutual fund industry. It was created to help solve your two main concerns: knowledge and trust.

First, what is a mutual fund? A mutual fund is a collection of stocks, bonds, or other securities owned by a group of investors and managed by a professional investment company. A mutual fund company is knowledgeable and experienced in selecting various types of securities based on the purpose of the fund. These professionals are licensed by the securities industry and have a fiduciary (legal or best effort) responsibility to use their expertise to make the best possible investments with your money. There are no guarantees, however, that their selections always will be profitable for you. However, over a long period of time, their records have been good.

The second concern—trust—is addressed by the Securities and Exchange Commission (SEC), the regulatory body that oversees the entire securities industry in the United States. Although bad things can still happen (fraud, cheats, and bad advice), the oversight by the SEC has been good for more than seven decades.

Mutual funds were established to address your concerns about the lack of knowledge and trust. The mutual fund industry is highly regulated by the government. The degree of transparency of both their results and their portfolios allows us to monitor their performance and stay informed about our investments.

Okay, so now let's have a more in-depth discussion about the mutual fund industry.

There are a lot of companies out there to manage your money. The types of mutual funds I'm about to describe may sound complex but they're not so confusing—and can be a lot of fun—once you get the hang of the terminology. If you'd rather put your trust in a good money manager and not worry about the details, that's okay too. Just make sure that the person and the company he or she works for are reputable.

There are people out there whose sole job is to manage your investments and provide tools to help you. It is their job to help you minimize the risk of individual stocks, explain your options, and help you keep track of your investments. Of course, nothing this good comes without a fee, but with this service, you have access to a lot of tools that will benefit you. In summary, if you pay these companies that provide these tools a little, you can get a lot of information and take fewer risks with your investments.

A mutual fund is a collection of stocks, bonds, and other types of investments, placed together in a portfolio. Each mutual fund is selected and managed by a financial organization like a bank or company that focuses on mutual funds. People new to investing, with little knowledge and experience, sometimes find mutual funds attractive because an expert is managing their money. When you buy into the fund, you own a share of it. This is similar to when you purchase stocks for a single company. You can make money from a mutual fund in two ways:

1. Earn income from dividends and/or interest

2. Earn profits from sales (when the fund sells something in its portfolio for a higher price than they bought it, or when you sell your shares in the fund for a higher price)

Although you can earn through income and/or appreciation, it's important to do your research about the advantages and disadvantages of different types of mutual fund investments.

Advantages of Mutual Funds

Mutual funds are convenient. An expert researches and analyzes the market and selects individual stocks to create the fund. This is someone who has experience in areas you may not be familiar with and who also understands the market. Although you don't have to actively manage your portfolio, you will still want to periodically review the portfolio and its results.

These funds are diversified; that means they include a variety of stocks (equity fund) or debt instruments (bond fund) and other assets, reducing the risk of loss and increasing the chance to achieve a positive return. This means that if one company in the fund doesn't do well, it won't destroy the entire portfolio. You aren't placing all of your eggs in one basket. There are so many different types of mutual funds that you can build a diverse portfolio without much difficulty and at little cost.

Mutual funds are invested according to the mandates of the fund (examples: invest only in growth stocks, maximize dividends or income, or invest in climate-friendly companies). These funds get volume discounts for buying and selling items in their portfolio. As a result, the fees they charge for managing the fund should be smaller than what you would have to pay to invest as an individual.

Mutual funds have years of experience supporting individual investors like you and have websites that help people keep track of their investments. This allows for transparency. All the information you need is publicly available. This enables investors to stay current, so they can make decisions that reflect their needs and risk profile.

Mutual funds are also liquid. That means you can easily buy into a mutual fund and leave it whenever you want, although you may have to pay a fee and adhere to any other policies the fund has in place. These entry and exit policies are readily available on the fund's website.

Another advantage of mutual funds is their low minimums. Many mutual fund companies have minimum initial investments as low as $100. Additions to some funds can be as small as $25, and no minimum amounts are required once the account is open. This gives you, the investor, the maximum flexibility to add money as you see fit. Also, if you prefer, there are plans that automatically deduct a certain amount from your checking account monthly.

In summary, you control the timing and amounts you wish to invest and decide in which funds you want to invest.

Disadvantages of Mutual Funds

The advantages of using mutual funds far outweigh the disadvantages. Knowing what to look for in a manager of a fund is both financially healthy and wise. For those with little investment knowledge or experience, mutual funds are a good way to get your feet wet. Like individual stocks, the value of mutual funds historically has gone up over time.

There are downsides, of course. First, you are paying someone else to manage your money. Experts, no matter how hard they try, can lose money or may be unable to keep their success at the same level over a long period of time. They aren't perfect, and they get paid whether your investment in their fund makes money or not. (Don't get me wrong—they have many incentives in place that make them want your portfolio to be successful—but things happen. There is risk in all investments.)

Another Disadvantage: Some funds charge fees or a "load" (commission) for using their funds. Some funds require a high minimum investment to start. These two things can make getting started inefficient and daunting. However, some of the largest mutual fund families in the world are "no-load" (no commission) with low expense ratios and high performance. Since this is a guide to getting started with small amounts of money, I will be showing you how to use no-load funds with only a small starting investment.

Some transactions made by a mutual fund manager (like selling a stock or sharing a dividend) may require you to pay taxes on money you receive. If a manager makes the decision to buy or sell the stock, resulting in tax consequences, you are responsible because it's your money. Again, the fund manager is maximizing the return on the fund, and your personal tax-planning needs unfortunately may not be in synch with his need to accomplish the fund's mandate.

When considering how to invest your money, consider all of the pros and cons, do your research, and choose based on your comfort level.

Now that you understand what a mutual fund is, let's look at the incredible array of investment possibilities available in the industry.

Types of Mutual Funds

There are three basic types of mutual funds you can choose from: equity funds, fixed-income funds, and savings or money market funds.

Equity Funds

These funds invest in stocks and are also known as stock funds. People invest in these funds when they are looking for long-term growth in value and some dividend income.

To help investors understand stocks and how they grow in value (or not), stocks are grouped into three categories: large cap, mid cap, and small cap. Market capitalization is the market value of a company's outstanding shares of stock.

Large cap funds invest in companies with large market capitalization (companies with values of $10 billion or more). Examples include Amazon, Coca-Cola, Google, and Facebook.

Mid cap funds invest in companies with a medium market capitalization (companies with values between $2 billion and $10 billion). Examples include Fresh Pet, Grey Television, and Skechers.

Small cap funds invest in companies with a small market capitalization (companies with values less than $2 billion). Examples include Unisys Corp., Northern Oil & Gas, and Magellan Health Inc.

Some funds will have a different mix of these types. Funds also differ in how the fund company manages its mix of stocks. For example, they can manage their portfolio for high growth or less-risky growth. When choosing an equity fund, you should keep these and other factors in mind. Remember that stock funds normally have higher growth but may have higher risk.

Fixed Income (Bond Funds)

Just like it sounds, these funds usually focus on providing a steady income to their investors—through dividend or interest rate payments, for example. Of the three types of mutual funds in this chapter, this one is somewhat conservative in risk. While bond funds pay more than money market funds (described below), they have some risk of losing value. Also, when interest rates go up in general, the value of a bond with a lower rate goes down. There are several types of fixed bond funds, including government bonds (the gold standard for safety), corporate bonds (higher return but more risk), and municipal bond funds with less risk than corporates and also certain tax advantages. All of these bond funds are managed conservatively and therefore usually have less risk and less return than an equity fund. Examples of bond fund holdings include Government National Mortgage Association, US Treasuries, and corporate bonds. All US government securities are considered the gold standard for their specific asset class.

Money Market

Of the three types of mutual funds in this chapter, money market funds are a low-risk, low-return place to put your money. They can be a good way and place to hold your cash either for liquidity or until you decide on your long-term investments.

When you invest in a money market account, the value of each share stays at one dollar. Your investment grows based on any interest earned, like a savings account, but with a higher interest rate.

One advantage of this type of mutual fund is that you can easily turn this investment into cash, which is why some people use money market accounts for short-term investing when they will need the money soon. Another advantage is that money market accounts have no loads (fees charged when you buy or sell shares in the funds). Money market funds can usually be redeemed within twenty-four hours, and many often invest in short-term overnight government securities (US Short-Term Government Treasuries).

One disadvantage of a money market fund is that the FDIC (Federal Deposit Insurance Corporation) does not insure your investment in the same way it handles savings and checking accounts. Though money market funds have a history of being safe and are regulated, this is something you should consider when choosing your investments. (Banks' deposits are insured up to $250,000 per account. Banks use their deposits to make loans and therefore generally have more risks for a depositor.)

More on Mutual Funds

My goal in the *Po Folks Investment Guide* is to introduce you to resources that can help you manage your money in a professional way while reducing your risk as much as possible. Mutual funds accomplish this. Very experienced and knowledgeable investors also use this tool to manage their money.

For some, this may be a good way to get started, but they may want more. While I have introduced you to mutual funds as an investment tool, I encourage you to explore and learn more if you wish. There are many books, seminars, webcasts, and other sources available to satisfy your thirst for investment advice.

Below are a few tips to help you with your mutual fund decision.

Some questions to ask about a mutual fund company:

- What is the fund's track record? How well has the fund done in the past five years?

- What fees are charged? When I join? When I leave? When I buy shares? When I sell shares?

- How does the mutual fund describe its goals? Growth? Value?

- How do they describe their approach to risk? Is this a high, medium, or low-risk fund?

The mutual fund industry has grown tremendously over the past thirty years. It has become very popular because of its positive results, ease of use, cost, and its lower risk for the average investor. As a result of this success, the number and types of funds have proliferated. There are now specific funds for almost every investment style and interest. Aside from equity, fixed-income, and money market, there other kinds of funds that might match your goals, risk profile, and interests. Here are some other types of funds for your consideration.

International/Global Funds focus on investments outside of the United States, which can be another way to diversify your portfolio.

Specialty Funds may only include companies that are socially responsible or are located in a specific part of the country.

Balanced Funds are mutual funds that have both stocks and bonds in their portfolios.

Index Funds have the value of their shares automatically tied to the overall stock market, which means that when the stock market goes up in value, so do your shares in the index fund. Also, your value goes down when the stock market goes down. An index fund invests in the stocks that compose the index like in the S&P 500 or some other general market measurement.

Exchange Traded Fund (ETF) is a type of security that involves a collection of securities—such as stocks —that often tracks an underlying Index, although they can invest in any number of industry sectors or use various strategies. ETFs are in many ways similar to mutual funds; however, they are listed on exchanges and ETF shares trade throughout the day just like an ordinary stock. Many ETFs have low initial investment requirements and low fees.

These are just a few more of the many types of funds available. Now that you know something about mutual funds, I challenge you to do your own research, especially if you're thinking that these funds may be for you. Look into the different types of mutual funds and their advantages and disadvantages. There are numerous kinds of funds (asset classes) and hundreds of different companies that can help with the management of your money.

To summarize, mutual funds are staffed by experienced, professional investment managers. Their fees are very competitive, they are easy to use, and their returns have been largely positive. You're in control of choosing who manages your funds and what types of funds you choose to invest in, including equity, bond, and money market.

In the next chapter, we will learn about mutual fund families, which are large companies that offer a variety of fund types, all managed by professionals with much experience.

It is not how much money you make—it's what you do with it that counts.

Chapter 9

Selecting Your Team

(Nepotism Encouraged)

In chapters 7 and 8, we discussed basic types of assets and how they have been grouped and managed as mutual funds by experienced professional investment managers.

My goal is not to turn you into a miniature investor extraordinaire like Warren Buffett, but rather to assist you, as a beginner, by helping you find money in your budget to invest, and guide you to select appropriate investments that match your goals, timeframe and risk profile.

Mutual funds offer many different asset classes, diversification, and low costs. They are used by individuals, wealth-management advisors, and many foundations and charities to manage their endowments. You may not have a large endowment, but your money is just as important, and you will need expert advice.

As of 2018, there were more than 9,500 mutual funds with assets totaling $17.7 trillion dollars. They are among the most popular vehicles for managing money. We've selected three funds as examples.

We'll use the Socratic Method of learning to help you decide which mutual fund is best for you. It's named after the ancient

Greek philosopher, Socrates, who was famous for asking questions to stimulate thinking and learning. Since the performance of any mutual fund varies over time, we'll teach you how to "fish" instead of giving you recommendations for a specific fund. This will enable you to refresh your portfolio as needed.

We'll use three different scenarios and walk you through some ways of thinking about each. Remember—these are for instructional purposes only.

First, ask yourself these questions before selecting a fund.

1. What are your investment goals?

2. What is your risk profile? Are you a risk-taker, or are you conservative? This will determine the percentage of your money in stocks (greater risk/return) or bonds (more conservative/less return).

3. What is your timeframe for a return on your investment? Five years, ten years, twenty years, or longer?

4. Are you investing for a source of income, such as bonds and dividends, or for an investment that may appreciate over a period of time, such as stocks, or both?

Now that you've thought about your investment goals, ask these questions for each fund you may be considering.

1. What are the investment strategies and goals of the fund?

2. How long has the fund existed?

3. Who are the fund's managers?

4. How has the fund performed compared to its stated objectives and industry benchmarks?

5. Are there fees?

6. What is the minimum you are required to invest to open an account?

7. How is the fund rated by rating agencies (Morning Star, Lipper)?

The first mutual fund, Massachusetts Investors Trust, was created on March 21, 1924, more than ninety years ago. Mutual funds have become a major part of most investors' portfolios and are used by both small and very large investment managers. Why? Because they work.

Large families of mutual funds have been created over the last fifty years and have become one-stop shopping for many investors. These fund families include funds for everyone from conservative investors to more aggressive, risk-taking clients. For those investors who want income, there is everything from short-term money market accounts to long-term bond funds and everything in between. There are even international stock and bond funds—all managed by professionals with many years of experience. For those who like one-stop shopping, balanced funds offer a mixture of both stocks and bonds.

These large fund families manage trillions of dollars in assets worldwide, and many have low expense ratios and requirements for opening an account. They can be a perfect fit for the beginning small investor.

In Exhibit 5 below, we list the top five (Asset Size) fund families as of December 2019. Although there are thousands of great mutual funds out there, we will be using only three of the top fund families as examples. They have many offerings, have online support (yes, real people), and have track records over many years, so the investor can see what their history of success has been.

The three fund families we will be using are Vanguard (Vanguard.com), T. Rowe Price (TROWEPRICE.com), and Fidelity (Fidelity.com). They have excellent records and are tracked by many rating agencies, including Morning Star and Lipper. They have both load and no-load funds, and you can easily move from one mutual fund to another within the fund family. Most of the funds have a competitive fee structure that keeps costs down and returns up. In addition, staying within a singular fund family (nepotism) when possible can reduce greatly the amount of administrative and research time.

Again, these three fund families are being used for illustrative purposes only. They will help demonstrate the thinking used to structure your beginning portfolio.

It is not how much money you make—
it's what you do with it that counts!

Exhibit 5
Top Five Mutual Fund Families
As of December 31, 2019

Rank	Family
1	Vanguard Group
2	Fidelity Management & Research
3	American Funds
4	T.Rowe Price
5	BlackRock Investment Funds

Chapter 10

The Easy Part

Buy right and hold tight.

—John Bogle, founder of Vanguard

We've explored mutual funds and questions to ask yourself and investment companies before you part with your money.

In this chapter, we select several funds and show how to build your first investment portfolio. Up to this point, everything we have discussed has given you the background to do this.

Our goal in this chapter is *not* to teach you how to select a particular mutual fund, but rather to provide a framework and methodology for evaluating any number of fund opportunities, ultimately selecting one or more funds that meet your needs. Since fund managers, asset classes (stocks, bonds, etc.), returns, and many other factors will change over time, we feel helping you establish a process for decision-making is much more important than our analyzing a particular fund.

So, let's get started. We offer three examples—**Saving For College**, **Setting Up a Retirement Fund**, and **Designing a Long-Term Nest Egg**.

Example 1—Saving for College

Mike is a thirty-five-year-old factory worker who has been with his current employer for seven years. His company has been in business for more than a half century and is a leader in its industry. Mike hopes to become a supervisor in the near future, knowing he'll get a raise.

Mike is married with three kids. His oldest is Brad, seven; he also has daughters who are five and two. His wife, Diane, is in junior college and hopes to get a part-time job.

It has always been Mike and Diane's intention to start an investment account to pay for college for their kids, but time slipped by, and they haven't saved a penny. With Brad only eleven years away from likely needing the money, his parents are determined to establish a college account.

Mike read in his local newspaper that college costs are increasing annually at a rate between 5 and 7 percent. He is relatively conservative. Diane is willing to take a little more risk. (Mike and Diane honeymooned in Vegas. Mike enjoyed the food and free entertainment, while Diane spent most of her time near the slot machines.)

WORKSHEET

Questions Mike and Diane Need to Answer

What is their goal?

It is to accumulate savings for their kids' education. Brad will start college in about a decade.

What is their risk profile? Risk-taker or conservative? This will determine the percentage of money they invest in stocks (greater risk/greater return) or bonds (less risk/less return). Mike is conservative, but Diane has been known to take some risk.

What is their timeframe?

The money will be needed in about a decade.

Are they investing for income or appreciation or both? Bonds are for income; stocks are for appreciation and growth. Mike and Diane are investing in funds that will increase in value over time; income is not needed now.

Summary

Mike and Diane require a conservative mutual fund that they expect may grow 5 to 7 percent yearly. This growth rate is typically associated with a stock mutual fund or exchange-traded fund. An exchange-traded fund is a marketable security that tracks a stock index, commodity, bonds, or a group of assets. Although similar in many ways, ETFs are different from mutual funds in that shares trade like common stock on an exchange.

Analysis

There are three basic types of stock mutual funds: Large-Cap (largest American corporations with at least $10 billion in value but with slower growth); Mid-Cap (companies that have $2 to 10 billion in value and grow faster than Large-Cap but with more risk); and Small-Cap (smaller companies with less than $2 billion in value, with fast growth but also with the most risk).

Let's look at each.

Large-Cap Funds are some of the nation's largest, most successful companies. With over $10 billion in value, their products are well known and successful. They are still growing but probably at a much slower rate. Examples of companies found in Large-Cap Funds are Apple, Inc.; Facebook, Inc.; Procter & Gamble Co.; and Home Depot, Inc.

Mid-Cap Funds (ETF) portfolios are composed of large, more proven companies that still may have considerable growth ahead of them. They also have a track record that suggests they may be a safer bet than Small Cap companies. Examples are Texas Instruments, Inc.; Southwest Airlines Co.; and Adobe, Inc.

Small Cap Mutual Fund (ETF) portfolios are usually composed of young, fast-growing companies. Some of the companies will continue to grow at a fast rate, while others may slow or go out of business at some point. Of the three groups, this category has the most risk. Examples include Zebra Technologies Corp.; Burlington Stores, Inc.; and DocuSign, Inc.

Selecting a Fund

One of PFIG's (PO Folks Investment Guide} goals is to teach the basics of value creation as clearly as possible. With that in mind, I mentioned in chapter 9 that there are large families of mutual funds. Three of the top most well-known funds (assets under management) are Vanguard, T. Rowe Price, and Fidelity. All of these large fund families have more than one hundred funds in their respective families. Some offer ETFs, and some do not. They all have websites, and most offer some type of online support. After screening all the websites, their product offerings, etc., I decided to choose Vanguard because it's one of the largest fund families with the most assets under management. Although all three (Vanguard, Fidelity, and T. Rowe Price) have very similar offerings, Vanguard was selected for the following reasons:

- They have funds for all major asset classes.

- They offer both traditional mutual funds and ETFs and require a low initial minimum investment.

- They have both online and telephone support.

- They have very low expense ratios.

For instructional purposes, it was easier to navigate one website as an actual example of how to select a fund, how to open an account, and how to track an investment. After you get some experience, you can later expand your research to the other two funds or to the more than five thousand funds available in the marketplace.

Example One: Setting Up a College Fund

Here's how Mike and Diane could immediately start saving money for college for their oldest son. We used **Vanguard. com**. (See exhibit 6.)

1. We could select traditional mutual funds or ETFs. We selected an ETF, primarily because Mike and Diane are just starting their investment portfolio. They needed to start with a minimum investment. For a traditional mutual fund, the minimum initial investment is $2,500 to $3,000. With an ETF, the initial investment can be as little as the price of one share of the fund, which is usually $100 to $300. We chose an equity ETF rather than a bond ETF because Mike and Diane need their money to grow, hopefully at least 5 to 7 percent per year to keep pace with college tuition costs.

2. We chose a Large Cap ETF. As one of the three major types of stock asset classes, Large Cap funds have the prospect of delivering more return but with the smallest amount of risk. Stocks in the fund are all old-line companies with proven products over many years.

3. On Vanguard.com, we reviewed a list of available Large Cap ETFs. We dropped all funds whose goals are *both* appreciation and dividends. We also eliminated any funds that were less than ten years old because they would not have given us a long performance history. (See exhibit 6-College Fund. All fund Information is for the period ending February 2019.)

4. Of the remaining funds, we selected the MGK Fund because it has a long-term, consistent performance record. Its annualized growth of 9.81 percent since inception is very competitive and exceeded all of the other Large Cap offerings. Although there are other funds with better five and ten-year returns, MGK was competitive both

at the five-year and ten-year timeframes. While past performance doesn't guarantee future performance, it's an indication of management's ability to perform against its stated investment objectives.

This fund has been in existence since December 17, 2007. Its average annual returns were: 1 year, 4.62%; 5 years, 11.73%; 10 years, 17.4%; since inception, 9.81%.

The expense ratio is a very low .07 percent. Morning Star gave the fund a four-out-of-five-star rating.

In summary, we wanted to find a fund that could provide an investment for Mike and Diane to help pay for their son's college education within a decade with a small initial minimum investment. Vanguard, as well as many other fund families, has offerings that fulfill this goal. An ETF was selected because of the low initial amount (approximately $120) needed to open an account, which they'll add to on a monthly basis. A Large Cap stock fund was selected because it has a history of annual returns over a ten-plus-year period that had exceeded the investor's stated goal. While it's impossible to be certain of future results, MKG has a track record of delivering an attractive return that, if replicated, would meet Mike and Diane's investment goals.

Exhibit 6
College Fund

Fund Name	Ticker Symbol	Asset Class	Expense Ratio	Price	Average Annual Returns as of 2/28/2019			
					1 Year (%)	5 Years (%)	10 Years (%)	Since Inception (%)
Vanguard Mega Cap Growth ETF	MGK	Stock-Large growth	0.07%	$120.36	4.62	11.73	17.4	9.81 (12/17/2007)
Growth ETF	VUG	Stock-Large growth	0.05%	$153.42	5.49	11.23	17.39	8.87 (1/26/2004)
Large Cap ETF	VV	Stock-Large growth	0.05%	$129.04	4.71	10.48	16.67	8.51 (1/27/2004)
Mega Cap ETF	MGC	Stock-Large growth	0.07%	$121.45	4.75	10.87	16.47	8.35 (12/17/2007)
Mega Cap Value ETF	MGV	Stock-Large growth	0.07%	$78.51	4.68	10.04	15.66	6.96 (12/17/2007)
Total Stock Market ETF	VTI	Stock-Large growth	0.04%	$257.84	5.1	10.14	16.85	7.06 (5/24/2001)
Value ETF	VTV	Stock-Large growth	0.05%	$108.29	3.93	9.81	16.02	7.98 (1/26/2004)
Dividend Appreciation ETF	VIG	Stock-Large growth	0.08%	$109.24	7.96	10.5	15.08	8.46 (4/21/2006)
ESG U.S. Stock	ESGV	Stock-Large growth	0.12%	$48.65	---	---	---	-3.12 (9/18/2018)
High Dividend Yield	VYM	Stock-Large growth	0.06%	$86.20	4.37	10.06	16.61	7.71 (11/10/2006)

Example Two- Setting Up a Retirement Account

Jeremy retired three years ago after taking a company buyout at age sixty-two. Recently, his father died, and Jeremy learned he would be getting $47,500 from his father's estate in one lump sum.

Jeremy and his wife, Hilda, own their home and live very frugally on his small company-paid pension and Social Security. Hilda quit her job years ago to raise their two kids. She receives a small check from Social Security that the couple uses to pay their supplemental healthcare insurance premiums.

Jeremy and Hilda could use more monthly income, but with rising costs, they also know that long term they will be unable to live only on Jeremy's pension and Social Security.

They are thinking about investing the inherited money long term in something that will not only supplement their monthly income but also may appreciate to at least keep pace with inflation.

WORKSHEET

Questions Jeremy and Hilda Need to Answer

What is their goal?

They want to invest long term to provide both income and appreciation.

Are they risk-takers or conservative?

This determines the percentage of money in stocks (greater risk/greater return) or bonds (less risk/less return).

Jeremy and Hilda are both in their mid-sixties and retired. They need the money for living expenses and cannot afford large risks. They want to invest conservatively.

What is their investment timeframe?

Five years, ten years, twenty years, or longer?

Jeremy's life expectancy is eighty-three; Hilda's is eighty-six to ninety years old, or approximately twenty years.

Are they investing for income, appreciation, or both?

Bonds are for income; stocks are for appreciation and growth. They need both, current income to supplement their pension and appreciation to keep their nest egg growing.

Summary

Jeremy and Hilda are retired, and life expectancy is from five to twenty years. The couple has a small pension and Social Security. They know they cannot make their Social Security and pension income last twenty more years if they do nothing or if they put the money into a low-yielding money market or savings account.

Analysis: There are three basic types of stock mutual funds: Large-Cap (largest American corporations with at least $10 billion in value but with slower growth); Mid-Cap (companies that have $2 to 10 billion in value and grow faster than Large Cap but with more risk); and Small-Cap (smaller companies with less than $ 2 billion in value, with fast growth but also with the most risk).

Let's look at each.

Large-Cap Funds are some of the nation's largest, most successful companies. With over $10 billion in value, their products are well known and successful. They are still growing but probably at a much slower rate. Examples of companies found in Large-Cap Funds are Apple, Inc.; Facebook, Inc.; Procter & Gamble Co.; and Home Depot, Inc.

Mid-Cap Funds portfolios are composed of large, more proven companies that still may have considerable growth ahead of them. They also have a track record that suggests they may be a safer bet than Small-Cap companies.

Small-Cap Mutual Fund portfolios are usually composed of young fast-growing companies. Some of the companies will continue to grow at a fast rate, while others may slow or go out of business at some point. Of the three groups, this category has the most risk.

Jeremy and Hilda need to be careful to manage their future inheritance. It has to last a long time, and its purchasing power has to be maintained. To accomplish this, they need a fund that will both have some appreciation and generate some current income. Jeremy and Hilda have decided to look at a balanced mutual fund. They can consider a regular mutual fund—they will have the $3,000 needed to open the account—or an ETF with its smaller initial requirement.

Using Vanguard.com, we did the following (see Exhibit 7 Retirement Fund).

1. **Select Traditional Mutual Funds or ETFs.** Since Jeremy and Hilda will receive $47,500 in a lump-sum payment, they have the minimum amounts necessary to open either a traditional mutual fund or an ETF. Both investments will be considered. (The minimum initial investment for a traditional mutual fund is $2,500 to $3,000; the price of one share in an ETF will be $100 to $300.)

2. **Select Asset Class**. We looked at both stock funds and bond funds, since they need appreciation (stock funds) and income (bond/dividend funds).

3. With a choice of Large-Cap, Mid-Cap, Small-Cap or bond funds, we selected Large-Cap, since those funds have the prospect of delivering more return with the smallest amount of risk. We also considered bond funds for income as well as balanced funds, which have a mixture of both.

4. We reviewed the list of all stock mutual funds (Large-Cap, Mid-Cap, and Small-Cap). We also looked at all stock ETFs (large, mid, and small-cap funds). In addition, we selected two balanced funds for review: Target Retirement Income (VTINX) and Managed Payout (VPGDX). See exhibit 7, Retirement Fund. Remembering Jeremy and Hilda's goal of supplementing their income for the next twenty years, they need both income (bond funds) and appreciation (stock funds). One way to accomplish that is to invest in both a stock fund and a bond fund. The ultimate investment

has to have both. Although the bond funds listed have good one, five, and ten-year returns, they do not have the appreciation (stock) factor that is also needed. We therefore could eliminate those two options. We could do the same with the stock funds, since they do not generate any meaningful revenue to help the couple with their monthly expenses. As you might imagine, Vanguard has created balanced funds (combined stocks and bonds) with different target dates to meet the needs of investors like Jeremy and Hilda. Those funds are composed of different percentages of stocks/bonds depending on the timeframe or other goals of the specific fund. Our two balanced fund selections have both stocks and bonds but varying percentages of each. We selected two balanced funds for review, which are the Target Retirement Fund (VTINX) and the Managed Payout Fund (VPGDX). Both are structured so that either would probably work for Jeremy and Hilda.

5. The Managed Payout Fund (VPGDX) is managed to pay out a set 4 percent per year and still maintain its value over many years. Some years that might not happen and there might be a dip into principal, but theoretically, the fund should meet its 4 percent payout goal over a long period of time. The Target Retirement Fund (VTINX) is also managed for income and appreciation. Since its inception, it has had an annual return of 5.09 percent vs. 4.83 percent for the Managed Payout Fund. Either fund would probably work for Jeremy and Hilda, but the Targeted Retirement Fund has performed slightly better. That fund is designed for people who have already retired, maintaining a 70 percent bond and

30 percent stock ratio. The stock portion is composed of five Vanguard Index Funds providing diversification over broad stock segments. Again, we should emphasize that past performance does not guarantee future performance, but it is an indicator of management's ability to perform against its stated investment objectives over a period of time.

6. For Jeremy and Hilda, we selected the Target Retirement Fund. As mentioned earlier, there are many funds like this from many fund families, as well as a number of individual funds.

Questions to Answer about Selected Fund

Fund Name: Target Retirement Income Fund (VTINX) as of 2/28/19

VTINX has five Vanguard index funds to provide current income and some capital appreciation. The fund holds approximately 30 percent of its assets in stocks and 70 percent in bonds. *This means that the fund will have income from the bonds and hopefully some appreciation from the stocks.*

The fund has been in existence since October 2003 and is managed by the Vanguard Equity Index Fund. Its average annual returns: 1 year, 2.38%; 5 years, 3.83%; 10 years, 7.02%; since inception, 5.09%.

The expense ratio is only 0.12 percent. The minimum amount needed to open an account is $1,000. Morning Star gives the fund, as of January 2019, three stars, with five stars the highest.

Summary

We searched for a fund that could deliver short and long-term funds for Jeremy and Hilda. Vanguard, as well as many other fund families, has offerings that fulfilled that goal. The goal of the Target Retirement Income Fund was to produce current income over a long period of time, while also achieving some capital appreciation. This fund is designed for investors who are already retired, and the minimum $1,000 initial payment was easily met by Jeremy and Hilda. This fund is a good fit for them.

Exhibit 7
Retirement Fund

Fund Name	Ticker Symbol	Asset Class	Expense Ratio	Price	Average Annual Returns as of 2/28/2019			
					1 Year (%)	5 Years (%)	10 Years (%)	Since Inception (%)
Vanguard Long-Term ETF	VGLT	Bond-Long term government	0.07%	$73.09	4.03	4.44	---	5.37 (11/19/2009)
Long-Term Bond ETF	BLV	Bond-Long term investment	0.07%	$87.41	2.18	4.51	6.77	6.27 (4/3/2007)
Long-Term Treasury	VUSTX	Bond-Long term government	0.20%	$11.58	3.71	4.29	4.96	7.29 (5/19/1986)
Target Retirement Income	VTINX	Balanced	0.12%	$13.26	2.38	3.83	7.02	5.09 (10/27/2003)
Managed Payout	VPGAX	Balanced	0.34%	$16.61	0.39	4.82	10.33	4.83 (5/2/2008)

Example 3--Building a Long -Term Nest Egg

Blair, thirty, is single and has worked for her current employer for several years; she feels confident about her future with the company. Blair has a great apartment, leases a BMW, and enjoys the nightlife. Her approach has been "If I want it, I get it." She's thinking "So far, so good."

However, lately, Blair has been thinking about her future. The $350 monthly lease on her BMW will end in a month, and she wonders about the economics of leasing a new car every two years. Some of her other financial decisions are also on her mind, like the vacations to the Bahamas and the New York trip she paid for with her credit card.

Blair recently met Rosemarie, forty-two years old, at her gym. She drives an eight-year-old car, shares an apartment with a roommate, and says she wants to be financially independent by the time she's fifty years old. This has some appeal to Blair as well, and she knows she can easily free up $200 to 250 a month and even more if she tries. She thinks being financially independent has a certain charm to it, and with a few changes in her spending habits, it may be an achievable goal for her. Blair asks Rosemarie for more details and also plans to seek investment advice.

WORKSHEET

Questions Blair needs to answer

She knows her goal is to accumulate enough assets to retire by the age of fifty. Blair has been happy-go-lucky when it comes to her savings. She would be a risk-taker if she were to put money in stocks (greater risk/greater return) and conservative if she were to invest in bonds (less risk/less return). She'd like enough money to retire within twenty years. She has the ability to invest long term for appreciation because she doesn't need the income now.

Analysis: There are basically three types of stock mutual funds. They are Large-Cap (largest American corporations with $10+ billion in value but slower growth; Mid-Cap (companies that have $2-10 billion in value and grow faster than Large-Cap but with more risks); and Small-Cap (smaller companies with less than $2 billion in value but have fast growth but most risk).

Large-Cap Funds are some of the nation's largest, most successful companies. With over $10 billion in market cap, their products are well known and successful. They are still growing, but probably at a much slower rate.

Mid-Cap Funds are composed of large, more proven companies that still may have considerable growth ahead of them. They also have a track record that suggests they may be a safer bet than small-cap companies.

Small-Cap Funds are usually composed of young, fast-growing companies. Some of the companies will continue to grow at a fast rate, while others may slow or go out of business at some point. Of the three groups, this category has the most risk.

Considering her tolerance for more risk, a twenty-year time-frame before the money is needed, and no need for supplemental monthly income, Blair has several options for reaching her goal by age fifty. She can invest with a Small-Cap

Fund for ten years and then reevaluate that investment when she's forty, or after ten years move to a Mid-Cap Fund (moderate growth/higher risk) or even a Large Cap fund (slow growth/less risk). A reassessment would be timely and may lead her to a different investment mix.

Using Vanguard.com (see Exhibit 8 Nest Egg Fund), we selected a Vanguard ETF. Since most of Vanguard's traditional mutual funds require a minimum of $2,500 to 3,000 to open an account, we were limited in our search to Vanguard's ETFs with a small initial amount required to open an account.

We looked only at stock funds, since Blair is interested in appreciation and growth of her investment dollars. Next, we had a choice of Large-Cap, Mid-Cap, or a Small-Cap fund. We selected Small-Cap Funds because they have the prospect of delivering more return, although with the greatest amount of risk (see Exhibit 8). Since Small-Cap Funds have the most risk (volatility and price fluctuations), twenty years is long enough to weather any downturns in the market while still capturing potential upside growth of her portfolio.

On Vanguard.com, we found Small-Cap Growth (VBK), a Small-Cap Fund with the highest return of the group at 18.6 percent (ten years). The next highest growth rate was a stock Mid-Cap Fund, Extended Market ETF (VXF), with a ten-year return of 17.71 percent. Third on the list with a ten-year average annual return of 17.4 percent is Mega Cap Growth ETF (MGK), a Large-Cap Fund.

Using Exhibit 8, the Inception column provides returns from the inception of each fund we examined. The fund with the highest return since inception is the Mega Cap Growth ETF (MGK) at

9.81 percent. This may be because it was the newest fund, starting in 2007, a time of one of the greatest stock market rallies in history. The other two funds were older (Extended Market ETF of 2001 and Small-Cap Growth Fund of 2004), which might explain this difference measured against the ten-year performance returns.

We selected the Small Cap Growth ETF (VBK) for Blair's investment vehicle.

Questions to Answer about Blair's Selected Fund

Fund Name: Small Cap Growth ETF (VBK) as of February 2019 (see Exhibit 8)

The fund seeks to match the performance of a diversified group of small-growth companies. The one we chose has been around since January 2004 and is managed by Vanguard Equity Index Fund. Its average annual returns: 1 year, 11.74 percent; 5 years, 8.16 percent; 10 years, 18.6 percent; since inception, 9.48 percent.

The expense ratio 0.07%.

The minimum amount needed to open the account was the price of one share—in this case $181.26. The chosen fund was given a four-star rating by Morning Star out of five stars.

Summary

We looked for a fund that would help Blair retire by the age of fifty. Vanguard, as well as many other fund families, has offerings that fulfill this goal. The fund we chose for the first ten years—the Small Cap Growth Fund ETF (VBK)—has a goal of producing growth and appreciation over a long period of time. The fund is designed for investors who have a long-term perspective and a risk profile that allows for some volatility in annual returns. The fund also requires a small initial payment to open an account (the price of one share). At the end of ten years, Blair can reassess and decide whether to stay with the Small Cap Growth Fund ETF (VBK) or switch to another fund that matches her risk and return expectations at that time.

These are three examples. Before investing in *any* fund, discuss your goals and expectations with the fund's representatives.

EXHIBIT 8
Nest Egg Fund

Fund Name	Ticker Symbol	Asset Class	Expense Ratio	Price	Average Annual Returns as of 2/28/2019			
					1 Year (%)	5 Years (%)	10 Years (%)	Since Inception (%)
Growth ETF	VUG	Stock-Large cap growth	0.05%	$153.42	5.49	11.23	17.39	8.87 (1/26/2004)
Large Cap ETF	VV	Stock-Large cap blend	0.05%	$129.04	4.71	10.48	16.67	8.51 (1/23/2004)
Mega Cap Growth ETF	MGK	Stock-Large cap growth	0.07%	$121.45	4.62	11.76	17.4	9.81 (12/17/2007)
Extended Market ETF	VXF	Stock-Mid cap blend	0.08%	$117.66	6.77	7.93	17.71	9.52 (12/27/2001)
Mid Cap Growth ETF	VOT	Stock-Mid cap growth	0.07%	$140.55	8.36	9.03	17.34	8.98 (8/17/2006)
Small Cap Growth ETF	VBK	Stock-Small cap growth	0.07%	$181.26	11.74	8.16	18.6	9.48 (1/26/2004)
Total Stock Market ETF	VTI	Stock-Large cap blend	0.04%	$144.41	5.1	10.14	16.85	7.06% (5/24/2001)

In this chapter, we presented three examples of long-term and short-term investor goals with different risk/return profiles. We walked you through how to think about selecting an appropriate fund for each situation. We selected one family fund (Vanguard) to use as an example for these case studies.

Vanguard has been in business for more than forty-five years, and they have a number of funds covering many asset classes that have performed well. They have very attractive expense ratios, and they offer both traditional mutual funds and ETF funds.

This same methodology and approach can be used to choose from any number of available fund families as well as many standalone funds. Each goal and each investor are different, and after mastering these techniques, it is the *Po Folks Investment Guide*'s hope that you will expand your searches to select the very best funds for your particular situation.

Although what we shared in this chapter is often the most sought-after information, it is also for some the most gut-wrenching part of making your first investment decision. *Po Folks Investment Guide*'s approach is to not only give you a methodology you can use to make your own decisions but also to present examples of funds and fund families.

We purposely repeated for each example the format and the descriptions of the various Mutual Funds and ETFs because we want you to use this as a checklist to help you cover the key areas needed for your analysis.

So, there you have it. You've seen how to think about and select the right funds for your investment needs. The professionals who manage these funds will do the rest.

It is not how much money you make—
it's what you do with it that counts!

Chapter 11

Unlike Love, This Isn't a One-Time Thing

Well, here we are. Ten chapters later, and what we've covered isn't rocket science—in fact, far from it.

Like many things in life, you look back and ask yourself, what is the big deal?

In life, big things often have very simple beginnings. Complexity is often viewed as difficult, and simplicity is overlooked many times as not having much, if any, value. After all, who is willing to pay for something that is simple vs. something difficult (even if it's made that way on purpose). Think legal contracts. Although they have legal underpinnings that are necessary, do they really have to be written in a manner that's totally incomprehensible to the average reader? May I suggest the wherefores, heretos and subparagraphs ad nauseam are there to create complexity, which then creates the need to pay someone to make it simple again?

In this final chapter, our goal is to summarize as simply as possible the few takeaways I hope you will keep, practice, and share with others.

Consumption vs. Investment

This is the number one takeaway from *Po Folks Investment Guide.* Minimize consumption and maximize investment. Spend money on the consumption items you need to live (food, shelter, clothing, etc.), but reduce those expenses whenever possible. Then switch as much of your money as you can to your investments bucket. Although this is not an absolute, while investments don't always go up in value, consumption items always go down. From this day forward, think about each and every dollar you spend. Which bucket should it go in and why?

Budgeting

Budgets don't always have to be in writing, but it's preferable that you at least make an annual list of your income and expenses. Certain items like rent or mortgage payments and car payments are fixed from one month to the next. Other recurring payments like utilities and food typically are predictable and can be estimated. Most other expenses are more controllable, such as going to the movies or restaurants or buying that dress or shirt that's on sale. Those often are unnecessary impulse buys or expenses.

Much like losing weight, by eliminating or reducing bad behaviors, you can cut wasteful expenditures and reduce the need for constant budgeting. You learn over a period of time what you need to eliminate to achieve your financial goals. These must-dos and must-don'ts should always be in the back of your mind.

Time and Compounding

Start early. How early is early? The day you were born is not too early! If you missed that date, try today. Seriously, the sooner, the better. As mentioned in chapter 6, Warren Buffett thinks the greatest financial formula ever created is compounding. That's when your money is making money for you. And then that money makes even more money for you and on and on and on.

I like to think that my investments never sleep. Starting to save sooner rather than later means that you arrive at your goals earlier. Some say compounding is the gift that keeps on giving. It's one of the few concepts that you never want to stop. It works with one dollar or with a million dollars. So get started.

Stocks, Bonds, and Mutual Funds

To refresh your memory, as a general rule, stocks have more risk than bonds because generally they return or increase in value more than bonds. Depending on your timeframe, risk profile, and goals, it may be wise to have both stocks and bonds in your portfolio.

It was never the purpose of this book to make you a professional money manager, but rather to show you how to accumulate money by first changing your spending habits and then understanding the basics of investing. Rather than introducing you to the many different types of financial instruments and trading techniques, we introduced you to a professionally managed, low-cost, diversified portfolio called a mutual fund.

To recap, mutual funds are managed by experienced investment professionals who have the expertise to select various asset classes (stocks, bonds, real estate, etc.) and invest your money prudently with your investment goals and timeframe in mind. Mutual funds offer a low-cost alternative (exchange-traded funds or ETFs) that operate just like mutual funds but often require a much smaller initial investment to open an account.

There are many types of mutual funds—both individually managed funds and very large families of funds (mutual fund families)—that offer a wide selection of asset classes, both domestically and internationally.

You may want to choose one of the larger fund families (like Vanguard.com, Fidelity.com, or TRowePrice.com) to get started. Then, as you become more knowledgeable and experienced, you can expand your portfolio of funds and fund advisors as you see fit.

Spread the Word about Wealth Creation and Giving Back

As you become more experienced and navigate your way to a more secure financial future, share that experience with others. When you discover some new savings opportunity or some new technique that helps you move more of your hard-earned money from consumption to investment, share that with others too.

If this system works as planned, your journey will not only help you, it will help others. It's with this sharing concept in mind that we have established **PoFolksInvestmentGuide.com**. It was set up so you can share your savings and financial tips with others and also learn from theirs. Like compounding, idea-sharing is not only a way to execute your own ideas but also allows you to grow your assets even faster by trying the successful ideas of others.

Whether you are Warren Buffett or the fellow or gal next door, wealth creation begins when you buy your first share of stock or first bond. From that point, you are not only working for money but letting that money work for you.

As you gain more financial freedom, I hope you will share not just your ideas but some of your financial rewards too. There are many churches, charities, and other nonprofits that need your help. They exist in every community, and you'll find that helping others is as worthwhile as any reward you'll find.

Remember, the longest journey begins with the first step. We hope we have helped you with a road map that will enable you to achieve the financial success you desire and deserve.

It is not how much money you make—
it's what you do with it that counts!

Postscript

Although Chapter 11 is the last chapter of Po Folks Investment Guide, it is the opening Chapter for PoFolksInvestment Guide.com.

Our website is to *Po Folks Investment Guide* followers as weekly Weight Watchers gatherings are to Weight Watchers enrollees.

In other words, it is the gathering place for the exchange of ideas as well as a booster forum to celebrate one's successes, no matter how large or small. (Remember in Chapter 4, we celebrated a savings of fifty cents on a single cup of coffee at McDonald's!)

Our spiritual and financial leader for the rest of this journey is none other than Dr. Pofix, a doctor whose specialty is fixing po. To visit with him in his office, please go to DrPofix.com. (PoFolksInvestmentGuide.com and Drpofix.com take you to his office, where he is available to help you improve your financial well-being!)

And don't forget to tell your friends and family members about DrPofix.com, and maybe, just maybe, they may also want to participate.

It is not how much money you make—it's what you do with it that counts!

Dr. PoFix's Definition of Big Terms

(Some People Call It A Glossary)

American Stock Exchange (AMEX)-The AMEX is the United States' second-largest floor-based stock exchange. In 1998, the AMEX merged with the Nasdaq to form the Nasdaq-Amex Market Group. To be listed, it requires pre-tax income of $750,000 for most recent fiscal year or two out of the most three recent fiscal years, a **market** value of public float of $3 million, an initial minimum bid price of $3 and stockholder's **equity** of $4 million.

Annual Report-A report issued each year by a public company that includes information about the company's business and its financial performance.

Asset-Anything that has monetary value and can be sold or converted into money. Typical personal assets include stocks, real estate, jewelry, art, cars, bank accounts, and antiques.

Blue-Chip Stocks-Stocks of established companies with strong records of rewarding shareholders. Examples include Caterpillar, Coca-Cola, Ford Motor Company, Johnson & Johnson, and Pfizer.

Bond-An interest-bearing or discounted debt security issued by corporations, governments, or others. A bond is essentially a loan made by an investor to an issuer.

Broker-One who sells financial products including real estate, commodities, insurance, stocks and bonds.

Capital-A business's cash or property, or an investor's financial assets.

Capital Gain/Loss-The difference between the proceeds from the sale of an asset and its original purchase price.

Capitalization-See Market Capitalization.

Cash Flow-The cash that flows through (i.e., is generated or used by) a company during a specified period.

Certificate of Deposit (CD)-An insured, interest-bearing deposit at a bank, requiring the depositor to keep the money invested for a specific length of time.

Commission-A fee charged by a broker for executing a transaction.

Common Stock-A security representing partial ownership in a corporation.

Compounding-Is the process in which an asset's earnings, from either capital gains or interest, are reinvested to generate additional earnings over time.

Crash-A market crash is a big drop in market value. It is what many shorter-term investors always worry about.

Discount Broker-A brokerage that executes orders to buy and sell securities at lower commission rates than a full-service brokerage.

Dividend-A distribution from a company to its shareholders from its earnings. Typically, dividends are paid on a quarterly basis.

Dividend Reinvestment Plan (Drip)-A plan permitting investors to invest small amounts of money in a company's stock, with the option of having dividends automatically reinvested in additional stock.

Dow Jones Industrial Average (Dow or DJIA)-The oldest and most widely known index of the stock market. The "Dow" represents the average of 30 actively traded major American companies. Examples include: Home Depot, Exxon, Coca-Cola and Disney.

Earnings-Earnings, also known as net income or net profit, are what is left over from revenues after a company covers all its costs and pays all its bills.

Exchange Traded Fund (ETF)-is a type of security that involves a collection of securities, such as stocks, that often tracks an underlying Index, although they can invest in a number of industry sectors or use various strategies. ETFs are in many ways similar to mutual funds; however, they are listed on exchanges, and ETF shares trade throughout the day just like ordinary stock. Many ETFs have low initial investment requirements and low fees.

Equities (Stock)-A name that comes from "equitable claims." Equities are just shares of stock. Because they represent a proportional share in a business, they are equitable claims on the business itself.

Expense Ratio-The percentage of a mutual fund's average net assets used to pay operating expenses-much of which goes to the salesmen and managers of the fund.

If you are investing in mutual funds, look for those with an expense ratio of less than 1%.

Federal Reserve-The central bank of the United States. The Federal Reserve (or "Fed") oversees money supply, interest rates, and credit. The Federal Open Market Committee (FOMC) is the 12-member policy-making arm of the Fed that sets monetary policy, chiefly by setting interest rates. It also buys and sells government securities, which increases or decreases the nation's money supply.

Fixed-Income Fund-A mutual fund that invests in bonds including U.S. Treasuries, corporate and municipal bonds.

Front-End Load-A sales commission charged by a mutual fund when the investment is purchased-typically around 3% to 5%. You can avoid this fee with no-load funds.

Full-Service Broker-Full-service brokers earn their name because they offer their customers not only executions of trades, but also investment guidance, research, and other services. For this, they have traditionally charged higher fees.

Income Fund-A mutual fund that invests in bonds and companies paying significant dividends.

Index-A selection of securities whose collective performance is used as a standard to measure the stock market. Some indexes reflect a specific sector, industry, or region. Examples include the Dow Jones Industrial Average, The Standard & Poor's 500, and Wilshire 5000.

Index Fund-A passively managed mutual fund that seeks essentially to duplicate the performance of a particular market index. It typically charges very low fees, compared to actively managed mutual funds.

Individual Retirement Account (IRA)-A tax-deferred retirement account set-up with a financial institution such as a bank or brokerage, in which contributions many be invested in many types of securities.

Initial Public Offering (IPO)-A company's first offering of common stock to the public.

Institutions-Institutional investors include pension funds, insurance funds, mutual funds, and hedge funds.

Liabilities-Outstanding debts.

Load-A sales fee or commission charges by some mutual funds when you buy or sell their shares. When a fund's (front-end) load is 5% for every $100 you invest, you are only getting $95 invested into the market, as $5 goes to the salesperson and/or mutual fund company. You can avoid loads by choosing no-load funds.

Market Capitalization (or "Market Cap")-A company's total stock market value, calculated by multiplying the current price of a single share of stock by the total number of shares outstanding. This can be viewed as proxy for the value of the company.

Money Market Fund-A mutual fund that invests in very-short-term, high-liquidity investments. Essentially akin to a savings account, though usually offering better interest rates than a passbook savings account.

Mutual Fund-An investment company that takes the cash of many shareholders and invests it in a particular way, as defined by the fund's prospectus. Examples include large cap, small cap, and international funds.

Nasdaq Stock Market-The Nasdaq began as the world's first electronic stock market, and today is the exchange where investors trade stock in more than 5,000 companies.

Net Income-Start with a company's revenues, subtract all expenses, and you will end up with net income, aka earnings. Net income is listed on a company's income statement.

New York Stock Exchange (NYSE)-The oldest stock exchange in the United States, this Wall Street center is the one frequently featured on television-with hundreds of traders on the floor staring up at screens and answering phones, ready to trade stocks on command from their firms.

No-Load Fund-A mutual fund that charges no sales commission, or "load".

Odd Lot-A number of shares that is fewer than 100. Trading in odd lots used to incur higher transaction fees. Today, with online computerized discount trading, buying and selling stock in odd lots may no longer involve higher transaction costs.

Penny Stock-This term is generally applied to stocks trading for less than $5 per share. Penny stocks are notorious for their volatility and riskiness.

Portfolio-All the securities holdings of an individual, an institution, or a mutual fund.

Price-to-Earnings (P/E) Ratio-The share price of a stock divided by its earnings per share (EPS) over the past year.

Principal-The original cash placed into an investment.

Prospectus-A legal document that provides information about a potential investment, such as its investment objectives and policies, past performance, risks, and costs.

Return on Equity (ROE)-Return on equity is a measure of how much in earnings a company generates in four quarters compared to its shareholders' equity. It is measured as a percentage and serves as one measure of profitability.

Revenues (Sales)-Revenues are monies that a company collects from customers in exchange for products or services.

S&P 500 Index (Standard & Poor's 500 Index)-An index of 500 leading publicly traded companies in the United States. The S&P is generally thought of as the best measurement of the overall U.S. stock market, though the Wilshire 5000 is a more complete index.

SEC-See Securities and Exchange Commission.

Sector-A group of companies with shared characteristics-usually operating in a common industry.

Sector Fund-A mutual fund that invests in a relatively narrow market sector. For example, technology, energy, the Internet, or banking.

Securities-A name for shares of stock, bonds, or other financial instruments.

Securities and Exchange Commission (SEC)-The federal agency charged with ensuring that the U.S. stock market is a free and open market. All companies with stock registered in the United States must comply with SEC rules and regulations, which include filing quarterly reports on how the company is doing. The SEC, headed by five appointed members, was created under the Securities Exchange Act of 1934.

Stock-An ownership share in a corporation. Each share is a proportional stake in the corporation's assets and profits. If you buy stock in a company, you own a share of the successes and failures of that business.

Ticker Symbol-An abbreviation for a company's name that is used as shorthand by stock-quote reporting services and brokerages. For example, Coca-Cola is KO, Amazon is AMZN, McDonald's is MCD and Disney is DIS.

Trade-The purchase or sale of a stock, bond, or other security.

Valuation-The determination of a fair value for a security.

Volatility-The degree of movement in the price of a stock or security.

Wall Street-The financial district in New York City and the street on which the New York Stock Exchange is located, although the term is used mostly to refer to the professional investing establishment.

Working Capital-The liquid or near liquid asset of the company. Take the total current assets and subtract the total current liabilities. This measure compares money the company has at its disposal to money it needs to pay out in the near future.

Appendix 1

Category	Budget	Actual	Difference	Notes
Monthly pay (after taxes)				
Other				
Total Monthly Income				
Flexible Expenses	**Flexible expenses** are costs that are easily changed, reduced or eliminated. Spending money on entertainment and clothing represent **flexible expenses**. Even **expenses** that must be incurred, such as a grocery bill, can be considered **flexible** because the amount spent can vary.			
Utilities				
Electricity/gas/phone				
Other				
Total Utility Expenses				
Food and Entertainment				
Groceries/dining out				
Other				
Total Food and Entertainment				
Transportation				
Gas/parking/tolls				
Other				
Total Transportation Expenses				
Children				
School/lessons/ clothing				
Other				
Total Children Expenses				

Personal				
Dry cleaning/personal grooming				
Other				
Total Personal Expenses				
Health				
Doctor's visits/ medications				
Other				
Total Health/Medical Expenses				
Savings/Other Expenses				
Savings (401k, IRA)				
Other				
Total Savings/Other Expenses				
Total Flexible Expenses				
Fixed Expenses	A fixed expense is "any expense that does not change from period to period," such as mortgage or rent payments, some utility bills, and loan payments. The amounts may vary slightly, but you know they are due on a regular basis.			
Housing				
Mortgage/rent/ insurance/taxes				
Other				
Total Housing Expenses				
Utilities				
Cable/internet				
Other				
Total Utility Expenses				
Health				

Insurance premiums				
Other				
Total Health/Medical Expenses				
Transportation				
Car payments/ insurance				
Other				
Total Transportation Expenses				
Loan/Other Payments				
Student loans/alimony				
Other				
Total Loan/ Other Expenses				
Children				
Child care				
Other				
Total Children Expenses				
Total Fixed Expenses				
Monthly Totals				
Total Monthly Income				
Total Monthly Expenses				
Difference